MW00389628

**HIGH INTEREST/
LOW VOCABULARY**

Paula

Building Comprehension
Grade 4
(Vocabulary Gr. 2)

The high-interest, low-vocabulary stories in this book feature diversified subject matter. The contents include:

- *Current personalities*
- *Popular sports figures and events*
- *Ghosts, monsters, and mysteries*
- *Visual and performing arts*
- *Disasters*
- *Excerpts from legends and mythology*
- *Amazing facts and wonders in science and nature*

The stories are written with a controlled vocabulary averaging two readability levels below the content. A male-female, ethnic, and geographic balance has been maintained in the selections. Follow-up questions reinforce key comprehension skills. These include: recognition of main idea, significant details, word meaning in context, inference, and drawing conclusions.

Thoughtful discussions and on-going projects can be generated from many of the stories. Where space permits, a follow-through activity has been included to lead to self-motivated reading or to valuable discussion, also allowing the teacher opportunity to award extra credit. Questioning format varies to avoid predictability.

Authors
Ellen M. Dolan
Sue D. Royals

Artists
Kathy Mitter
Lee Brubaker

Copyright © 1999
Milliken Publishing Company
a Lorenz company
P.O. Box 802
Dayton, OH 45401-0802
www.LorenzEducationalPress.com

MP3388

Table of Contents

Teaching Guide

Introduction

This book is one of six in a series designed to encourage the reading enjoyment of young students. Subject matter was carefully chosen to correspond to student interests. Skills were selected to reinforce understanding of the readings and to promote confidence in independent reading.

Content

The contents of each book have been drawn from seven specific categories: 1) biography, 2) amazing facts, 3) mystery and intrigue, 4) sports stars and events, 5) visual and performing arts, 6) wonders in science and nature, and 7) excerpts from mythology and literature.

The popular biographies, sports figures, and artists give students an opportunity to identify with people who are familiar to them. Those figures who are unknown to the students' experience give them clues to the wide diversity of current society in many countries. A look behind the scenes of a famous life holds a never-ending fascination.

In addition to spy stories and tales of ghostly encounters, the mystery selections often offer a puzzling situation to solve or the beginning of a story which must be completed by the reader.

Science and nature selections are chosen to generate interest in new and untapped areas of the readers' knowledge and to encourage them to explore further.

Samples of a wide variety of stories from mythology and literature have been included. It is hoped that this brief encounter with some of the great story lines will motivate the student to seek out and read the entire selection.

Skills

The skills employed in this series are drawn from traditional educational objectives. The five comprehension areas practiced in this series are: main idea, recognition of significant details, use of context clues for determining word meaning, inference, and drawing conclusions. All categories are not necessarily represented at the conclusion of each story. Questioning format varies from book to book to avoid predictability. Where space permits, a follow-through activity has been included. These are expected to lead to self-motivated reading or to valuable discussion. The activity also gives the teacher an opportunity to award extra credit.

Upon completion of each collection of stories and accompanying skill activities, students should show improvement in the areas practiced; i.e., the ability to locate, evaluate, and predict, as well as to conduct study and research.

Readability

The reading level of each book is essentially two years below the interest level. Readability levels were confirmed by the Spache formula for the lower grades and the Dale-Chall formula for the upper grades. Each book is suitable for a variety of students working at a range of reading levels. The lower readability allows older students with reading deficiencies to enjoy high-interest content with minimum frustration. The comprehension activities provide a growth opportunity for capable students as well. The high-interest content should help to motivate students at any level.

The teacher should keep in mind that supplying easy-to-read content provides a good setting for learning new skills. Thus, comprehension development can best take place where vocabulary and sentence constraints ensure student understanding. It should be obvious that the concept of main idea, as well as the nature of an inference, can be seen best where the total content of a selection is well within a reader's grasp.

Finally, the material is dedicated to the principle that the more a student reads, the better he or she reads, and the greater is the appreciation of the printed word.

Answer Key

Page 1
1. b
2. a
3. b
4. a
5. c
6. b

Page 2
1. b
2. a
3. c
4. b
5. a

Page 4
1. c
2. b
3. *Cricket* magazine
4. a
5. c
6. b

Page 5
1. a
2. a
3. a
4. c
5. c
6. false
7. false
8. true

Page 6
1. b
2. false
3. false
4. true
5. b
6. prize
7. c

Page 7
1. a
2. c
3. a

4. c
5. a
6. c

Page 8
1. b
2. a
3. b
4. b

Page 9
1. snake or python
2. b
3. c
4. a
5. a
6. false
7. true
8. true

Page 10
1. c
2. mirror
3. island
4. b
5. a

Page 12
1. a, c, f
2. c
3. b
4. c
5. quiet
6. c

Page 14
1. large piece of ice floating in ocean
2. piece of glacier breaks off
3. glaciers
4. hardens and turns to ice
5. in cold oceans
6. a group to watch for icebergs
7. b
8. any 2—radar, airplanes,

satellites
9. a
10. b
11. Sink ships. Bottom of iceberg cannot be seen underwater.
12. Icebergs made of ice. Must be in cold places to stay solid.
13. Yes. Not one ship lost to an iceberg.

Page 16
1. shipwreck
2. c
3. b
4. a
5. a
6. b
7. more lifeboats
8. Accept reasonable answers.

Page 18
1. b
2. c
3. a
4. c
5. b
6. c
7. a
8. c
9. a
10. Accept reasonable answers.
11. Accept reasonable answers.

Page 20
1. b
2. the ocean
3. flower called *toka*
4. mountains
5. rice straw
6. snow
7. b
8. a
9. c

iii

Page 22
1. c
2. Knew smoke would bring villagers.
3. grandfather
4. sea
5. rolled back
6. Ojiisan's grandson
7. ran to help
8. tidal wave
9. b
10. a

Page 23
1. c
2. a
3. c
4. b
5. b
6. c

Page 25
1. c
2. b
3. a
4. a
5. c
6. b

Page 26
1. a
2. b
3. b
4. a
5. c
6. b

Page 27
1. b
2. c
3. a
4. c
5. b
6. b

Page 29
1. c
2. a

3. c
4. b
5. c
6. b
7. c

Page 31
1. c
2. b
3. c
4. a
5. c
6. b

Page 33
1. c
2. b
3. b
4. a
5. c
6. c
7. a

Page 35
1. c
2. a
3. b
4. c
5. a
6. a
7. b

Page 37
1. a
2. c
3. b
4. a
5. b
6. c
7. a

Page 39
1. a
2. c
3. b
4. b
5. a
6. c

Page 40
1. b
2. a
3. c
4. a
5. c
6. b

Page 41
1. c
2. a
3. c
4. b
5. a
6. a

Page 42
1. a
2. b
3. c
4. a
5. a

Page 43
1. b
2. a
3. c
4. b
5. b
6. a
7. Accept reasonable answers.
8. Accept reasonable answers.

MP3388

Jim Davis

Everyone knows Garfield. He is the fun-loving, fat cat in the comic strips. People all over the world like to read about the orange-and-black striped cat.

But who made Garfield? Jim Davis is the cartoonist who writes the Garfield comic strips. When Jim was a young boy, he was sick with asthma. He had to stay in bed a lot. He wanted something to do, so he drew pictures. People laughed at his pictures. Jim put words with his pictures and people laughed harder. Jim read other comic strips. He saw that there were many dogs in the comics, but no cats. That is how he got the idea for Garfield.

But Garfield is no ordinary cat. Garfield hates to eat mice. He likes to eat lasagna. He likes to kick Odie, the dog in his comic strip. Sometimes Garfield likes to cause trouble, but he always has fun.

Jim has fun writing about Garfield. Jim thinks that drawing a comic strip is like telling a joke. But Jim works hard, too. He takes time to draw Garfield's body just right. Jim even formed a company called Paws, Inc. to make sure that every picture of Garfield is perfect. This careful work has made Garfield very popular.

Now everyone in the world can watch or read about Garfield. Jim has won many awards for his comic strips, posters, books, and TV shows about the funny, furry Garfield.

Main Idea

1. Jim Davis
   a. is a cat.
   b. writes the Garfield comic strip.
   c. is a young boy.
2. Jim Davis must _____ at his job.
   a. write and draw
   b. sing and dance
   c. give medicine to sick children

Significant Details

3. Garfield likes to eat
   a. mice.
   b. lasagna.
   c. cat food.
4. Jim formed the company Paws, Inc. to
   a. make sure the drawings of Garfield were just right.
   b. do all the work on the comic strip.
   c. make movies about Garfield.

Context Clues

5. Jim Davis is a *cartoonist.*
   a. person who reads comic strips
   b. person who works at a bank
   c. person who writes comic strips
6. Garfield is not an *ordinary* cat.
   a. orange
   b. plain
   c. large

Drawing Conclusions

7. How does Davis feel about cats?

Monsters on the Roof

Would you be surprised if you saw a monster in church? In days gone by, almost every church roof in Europe had a large scary monster on each corner. They were carved from stone and called "gargoyles." Many people believed these monsters would frighten away evil spirits. But the gargoyles did have a real use.

In those times, there were no gutters on the roofs to carry away water. So when it rained, water ran down the sides of the buildings. The rocks turned brown and the ground got very wet. Builders began to put long pipes on the corners of the roof. They stuck out about three feet from the building. This looked very ugly. So they began to hide the pipes under the stone carvings.

"Gargoyle" means throat. The pipe ran through the stone monster's throat and poured the rain water out of its mouth. It fell far from the side of the building. Most of the gargoyles were mean and scary looking. But sometimes the carver had a little fun. The monsters might end up looking like a friend. Or sometimes it might be an enemy. Today gargoyles are just decoration. But it is sometimes hard to look at them without giving a shiver. Do they still keep evil spirits away?

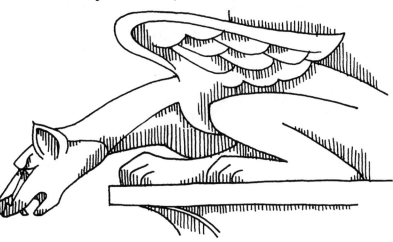

Main Idea

1. This story is mainly about
   a. rain.
   b. stone carvings.
   c. pipes.

Significant Details

2. Gargoyles are often seen on
   a. roofs.
   b. wet ground.
   c. stones.

3. The word "gargoyle" means
   a. church.
   b. friend.
   c. throat.

Context Clues

4. A *gargoyle* is something like a
   a. building.
   b. statue.
   c. rock.

5. To *frighten* means to
   a. scare.
   b. send help.
   c. scold.

Drawing Conclusions

6. Did gargoyles help most with evil spirits or rain run-off? Explain your conclusion. _____
   _____
   _____

Following Through

7. Look around your own town or city for decorations on buildings. Describe something that you find, and tell about its uses. _____
   _____
   _____
   _____
   _____

Who Are They?

Inez was in a hurry. The first class this morning at her new school was science. The teacher was going to talk about flying saucers. Of all the things in science, Inez liked flying saucers best. She must not be late today. Inez picked up her books and called good-bye to her family. She ran out the door and down the street.

At the first corner she stopped. She knew it would be faster to turn right, but she had never gone that way. What should she do? Go the usual way and be late or try a new way and be on time? She turned the corner and kept running. Suddenly two figures jumped from a doorway and stood in front of her. One was dressed all in green and the other in black. The green one said, "At last! We have been waiting so long for you."

Finish the story. If necessary, continue on another paper.

_____

_____

_____

_____

_____

_____

3

MP3388

Trina's Magic Fingers

Trina Schart Hyman could always find some kind of fairyland. When she was small, she lived near a farm. The queen of her first fairyland was the farmer's wife, who sold her eggs. When Trina was older, she often went to Philadelphia with her father. Here was another fairyland: the art museum filled with paintings. Trina had "friends" among the paintings there. Each time she visited there, she went to look at these friends and learn from them.

When Trina finished high school, she went to art school. There was the best fairyland of all. She could draw all day long. No one said, "Stop that scribbling. Get to work." She *was* working.

After art school, Trina married. She and her husband went to Sweden for a few years. In that fairyland of trolls and elves, Trina illustrated her first children's book. Since then, she has drawn beautiful pictures for many, many books. Her drawings are always full of wonderful little details. She

pulls the reader further and further into the world of make-believe.

Then came a new children's magazine, *Cricket*. Trina was asked to be the art director. She still illustrates books. But now she also works with other artists. She is leading them into that fairyland she knows so well. It is called — imagination.

Main Idea
1. The story is mainly about
   a. farms.
   b. a new magazine.
   c. an artist.

Significant Details
2. Trina's friends at the art museum
   a. were artists.
   b. were her favorite paintings.
   c. were her teachers.
3. Trina was asked to be art director of _____ .

Context Clues
4. To *illustrate* means the same as to
   a. draw.
   b. marry.
   c. visit.
5. The *fairyland of imagination* is
   a. your television set.
   b. your hometown.
   c. your mind.

Drawing Conclusions
6. It is easy to guess that Trina
   a. is bored by her work.
   b. loves her work.
   c. dislikes her work.

Madurodam

Madurodam is the smallest town in Holland. When you walk down its streets, you can look down on the tops of the buildings. Madurodam and everything in it is doll-sized. The town was built for children, but grown-ups like it, too. This miniature town has everything that a life-sized city in Holland has. Tiny boats sail in the water. Toy trains run down the tracks. There are little windmills that really work. The miniature buildings are beautiful. Some buildings even have towers with tiny clocks. There are little stores, schools, forests, and factories. At night, the town of Madurodam looks very beautiful. After the sun goes down, 50,000 lights are turned on in the city. Then there is a tiny parade through the streets. It is led by a queen's Golden Coach. A band plays music.

The town of Madurodam was built by the Maduro family. They built it to honor their son, George, a Dutch soldier who was killed in World War II. All the money that visitors pay to see the town goes to projects and schools for the children of Holland. The town not only gives enjoyment to the children when they are young, but helps pay for school when they are older.

Main Idea
1. The main idea of this story is:
   a. Madurodam is a tiny town built for children to enjoy.
   b. Holland is the smallest country in the world.
   c. At night there is a parade in the town of Madurodam.

Significant Details
2. The town of Madurodam was built by
   a. the Maduro family.
   b. a Dutch soldier.
   c. the children of Holland.
3. Money from the visitors of Madurodam goes to
   a. schools in Holland.
   b. the Dutch soldiers.
   c. Madurodam.

Context Clues
4. The *miniature* town has everything a real town has.
   a. beautiful
   b. building
   c. tiny
5. *Grown-ups* enjoy Madurodam as much as their children do.
   a. partners
   b. visitors
   c. adults

Drawing Conclusions
6. T F Madurodam would be a good place to live.
7. T F Children can go to school in Madurodam.
8. T F A ten-year-old boy would not fit inside a house in Madurodam.

5

MP3388

The Eagle and the Finch
(Adapted from a Native American legend)

Sitting around an Ottawa campfire, you might hear this story. One day all the birds in the woods had a meeting. They wished to have a test. It would show which of all birds was the strongest. The bird that could fly the highest would win the prize.

At once all the birds took off. Soon all could see that the eagle had passed the others. He seemed to be heading for the sun. The eagle was sure he was winning the prize. But look! Hidden on the eagle's back was the finch, a small bird. She had come this far on the eagle to save her strength. At last the finch left the eagle's back and flew higher and higher. She was not tired at all.

When all the birds were back on the ground, they had to pick a winner. They gave the prize to the eagle. Not only did he fly highest, but he did it while carrying another bird on his back. He was the strongest.

From then on, the eagle's feather was always given to the best warrior in the tribe. It was to show that he was strong and brave.

Main Idea
1. This story is about a
   a. feather.
   b. race.
   c. campfire.

Significant Details
2. T   F   The finch was the winner.
3. T   F   The finch could not fly.
4. T   F   The finch was small.

Context Clues
5. A *warrior* is one who
   a. catches eagles.
   b. is a brave fighter.
   c. wins races.

6. The *winner* gets the _____ .
7. A *test* shows who is
   a. sitting.
   b. flying.
   c. best.

Following Through
8. The American bald eagle is the national symbol of the United States. Find out why. What else in this story suggests why the eagle was chosen? _____
_____
_____

© Milliken Publishing Company

Washoe

"Monkey see, monkey do." This old saying has a lot of truth in it. Monkeys are great imitators. They copy many things people do.

Scientists knew this about monkeys. They wanted to teach monkeys to talk. But monkeys do not have the same vocal cords as people. They are not able to actually "talk." But scientists thought that monkeys could learn American Sign Language. ASL, or American Sign Language, is a way deaf people in America communicate. Because hands and fingers are used in ASL, scientists knew that a monkey could copy it.

Washoe, a newborn chimpanzee, was picked for the experiment. Washoe lived in a laboratory with her trainers. Everyone who came into the laboratory had to use ASL. Soon Washoe could copy the hand movements her trainers used.

When Washoe learned the sign for "open," she used it often. "Open food" meant she wanted something from the refrigerator. "Open key" meant Washoe wanted to get through a locked door. The trainers laughed when Washoe signed "open faucet" so she could get a drink of water.

By the time Washoe was five, she could use over 80 ASL signs. She surprised her trainers one day with a sentence, "Listen, dog." Indeed, there was a dog barking outside, although Washoe couldn't see it.

Washoe learned many more signs and added them to her vocabulary. She became the first nonhuman animal to learn human language. Washoe even taught her adopted "children," Moja, Tatu, Dar, and Loulis how to sign. Now all the chimps communicate with each other and with humans.

The chimps live happily together at a university in Washington. Scientists and students can study the chimps. This work has taught scientists how to help some nontalking human children learn to communicate. Scientists agree that it is exciting to communicate with animals.

Main Idea

1. Animals and people can
   a. communicate with each other.
   b. dance with each other.
   c. eat the same food.

Significant Details

2. ASL uses
   a. vocal cords.
   b. hands and feet.
   c. hands and fingers.

3. Washoe is a
   a. chimpanzee.
   b. gorilla.
   c. tiger.

4. Washoe can
   a. talk.
   b. read a book.
   c. use sign language.

Context Clues

5. Monkeys *imitate* what people do.
   a. copy
   b. make fun of
   c. communicate

6. Washoe learned to *communicate* with others.
   a. imitate people
   b. play with others
   c. tell your thoughts to others

Joy Riding

Horse racing is fun to watch. Some races are on tracks and fields. But steeplechase racing is harder. There is no track in steeplechasing. Horses and riders run through the country. They go up hills and down. They jump rivers and fences.

Joy Slater of Pennsylvania raced in steeplechases since she was a child. Her grandmother and mother, both also named Joy, helped her. They taught her to ride. They helped train the beautiful horses that Joy would race. But it was Joy alone who had the determination to become a fine rider. She was up every morning before the sun. She practiced riding. She trained her horses. She listened carefully to her instructors. Soon she was a rider who could race, jump, and show horses.

In 1980, Joy entered the most difficult of the U.S. steeplechases, the Maryland Hunt Cup. She had to race through rough country. There were slippery, damp places on the ground. Joy rode her horse carefully through the bad places. She and the horse had to jump 22 fences. Joy concentrated very hard before each fence. She had to make the horse leave the ground at just the right time. At last the finish line was ahead. As she crossed the finish line, Joy became the first woman in history to win this big race!

Joy won the race again the next year. She went on to win many races around the world. Joy married a fellow horse racer named Rusty Carrier. Together, the two opened their own horse-racing training camp called *Fat Chance Farm.* There, they help train others for steeplechase racing. Anyone that comes to the farm can see that Joy and Rusty love horses!

Main Idea
1. This story is mainly about
   a. grandmothers.
   b. horse racing.
   c. Pennsylvania.

Significant Details
2. The hardest type of horse racing is
   a. steeplechase racing.
   b. track racing.
   c. open-field racing.

Context Clues
3. When Joy *concentrated,* she was
   a. pulling the reins.
   b. thinking hard.
   c. watching the horses.

Drawing Conclusions
4. After the steeplechase race, Joy was
   a. crying.
   b. tired but happy.
   c. angry.

Following Through
5. Read more about different kinds of horse races. Write about the history of one race or one horse.

Dinner for Two

Some people think it is cruel to cage animals in a zoo. But many animals would not last in the wild. Their homes may be lost to new building or bad floods. Often they cannot find food. Or they might need other help. In a Florida zoo, an unusual two-headed snake keeps helpers busy. It is a small python with a big appetite.

Pythons may eat only once a week. They find small animals and squeeze them until they cannot breathe. Then, the python swallows them whole. It takes some time for that kind of dinner to digest. When a two-headed snake eats at a zoo, the helpers put a board between the two heads. This way, one head cannot see the other's food. Sometimes one of the heads wants to go right and the other one pulls left. The snake may hurt itself and spend some time in the zoo hospital.

Such a snake would not live long in the woods. It would have trouble finding and killing animals for food. It could be hurt by larger animals. And, without the zoo, people might never get to see this interesting bit of nature.

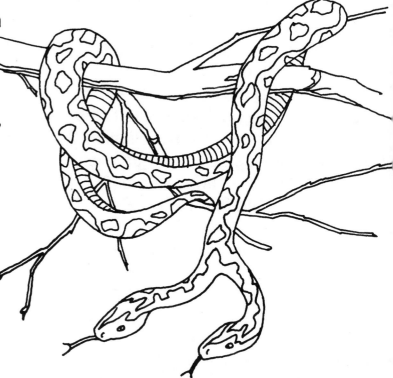

Main Idea
1. This story is about a _____ .
Significant Details
2. A python eats
   a. once a day.
   b. once a week.
   c. once in a while.
Context Clues
3. If a python has a big *appetite,* it is
   a. hurt.
   b. large.
   c. hungry.
4. This *unusual* snake is
   a. rare.
   b. normal.
   c. found in large numbers.

5. It takes some time for dinner to *digest.*
   a. break down for energy
   b. spoil
   c. die
Drawing Conclusions
6. T F Zoos do not help animals that are hurt.
7. T F There are not many two-headed snakes.
8. T F Snakes can be seen in a zoo.
Following Through
9. Some animals, such as pandas, are hard to keep in zoos. Choose one wild animal and write about the problems of keeping it in a zoo.

Medusa
(Adapted from Greek Mythology)

Perseus and his mother lived on a beautiful Greek island. The evil king of the island wanted to marry Perseus' mother. And at the same time, he wanted to get rid of Perseus. So he asked Perseus for a present. Perseus did not know it was a trick and said yes. The king then asked for the head of the monster Medusa. Too late did Perseus find out his mistake. But he would not back down. He would find Medusa and bring her head to the king.

Friends helped Perseus to get ready. They gave him useful things. One gave him a magic sword. Another gave him a bag to carry Medusa's head. Best of all was a shield, which was as polished and shiny as a mirror. Perseus was ready. He put on magic sandals. In no time, he landed in Africa where Medusa lived.

Medusa had once been beautiful. Now her hands were claws and her hair was a nest of hissing snakes. Her face was so terrible that anyone who looked at it would turn to stone. So Perseus was careful to look into the shiny shield as he moved close to her. He was very quiet. Then quick! He swung the sword and cut off her head. With the snakes still hissing, he dropped Medusa's head into the bag.

When he got back to the island, the king could not believe that he had killed Medusa. So Perseus opened the bag. The king looked at her head and at once turned to stone. Perseus had killed a terrible monster. He had ended the life of an evil king. And he had saved his mother. His new name became the "Destroyer."

Main Idea
1. Choose the most important fact in the story.
   a. Perseus was a Greek.
   b. Medusa had once been beautiful.
   c. Perseus killed Medusa.

Significant Details
2. Perseus used the shield as a

   _____ .

3. Perseus lived on an _____ .

Context Clues
4. *Sandals* are a kind of
   a. sword.
   b. shoe.
   c. hat.

Drawing Conclusions
5. Perseus did not wish the king to
   a. marry his mother.
   b. get a present.
   c. turn to stone.

Following Through
6. Perseus is one of the heroes in Greek mythology. Find out about other monsters he killed. Was "Destroyer" a good name for him? Explain.

MP3388

Jacques Cousteau

Most people know about the Baseball Hall of Fame. There is also a Cowboy Hall of Fame. Another important hall is the Hall of Fame for Environmentalists. The people in it have done many things to help protect and preserve our planet. One of the first people to be in this hall of fame was a Frenchman. He was Jacques Yves Cousteau, a famous explorer. Cousteau explored the world underwater. He loved the beautiful plant and animal life deep in the sea. He began to take pictures underwater. For the first time, people began to see what wonderful things live and grow in that part of our planet.

Cousteau explored almost every possible thing underwater. He found sea creatures, strange plants, and buried treasure. Soon the things Cousteau saw were being shown to everyone once a week on his TV show. Cousteau could write as well as swim. His book *The Silent World* was so good that it was made into an award-winning movie.

Cousteau invented the aqualung or S.C.U.B.A. It is a tank filled with air. Divers carry it on their backs when they go underwater. They can stay under-water for a long time. He invented many other tools and ideas for use underwater.

Cousteau was worried about the future of our oceans and seas. He began speaking to people about how to save our seas. He told them not to dump garbage in the sea. He told factories not to put their wastes into the oceans. And he told other divers to be careful of the underwater plants and animals when they are diving.

Jacques Cousteau was voted the "most-loved" man in France. People still felt that way when he died in 1997 at the age of 87. Cousteau's work still goes on. Other environmentalists want to save the seas and oceans, too. The Jacques Cousteau Foundation was started. All the workers in the Foundation try to follow Cousteau's footsteps. They work hard to save underwater life. Because of Cousteau and his workers, the colorful undersea world should be around for many generations to come.

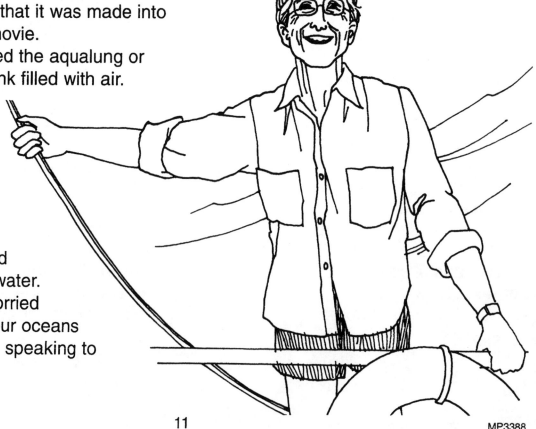

Main Idea

1. Cousteau is *(circle all that apply)*
   a. a writer.
   b. a cowboy.
   c. an underwater explorer.
   d. a young man.
   e. a South American.
   f. a photographer.

Significant Details

2. Underwater, Cousteau has found
   a. baseballs.
   b. maps.
   c. buried treasure.

Context Clues

3. When a man is *famous,* he is
   a. old.
   b. well-known.
   c. French.

4. *Exploring* is the same as
   a. giving parties.
   b. inventing tools.
   c. looking for things.

5. *Silent* means _____.

Drawing Conclusions

6. Cousteau was probably most proud of
   a. his underwater pictures.
   b. his life in France.
   c. his work saving life under the sea.

Icebergs

Icebergs are large pieces of ice in the ocean. The word "berg" means mountain. These "mountains of ice" are big and beautiful. Some weigh one million tons. One iceberg is two times bigger than the state of Rhode Island.

Icebergs are beautiful to see but they can be dangerous. Ships must be careful of icebergs. Icebergs are bigger underwater than on top of the water. Sailors on the ships cannot see under the water. Their ship might run into an iceberg before anyone can see it. Years ago many ships were sunk because they hit an iceberg. Sailors hated icebergs.

Icebergs are born from glaciers. There are places near the Antarctic, North Pacific, and North Atlantic Oceans that are cold all year long. In some places it snows every day. After a few years, the snow is packed so hard that it turns to ice. White rivers of ice begin to flow towards the sea. These rivers of ice are glaciers. It takes many years for a glacier to get to the sea. When a glacier meets the ocean water, it begins to melt. Soon a huge chunk of ice breaks off from the glacier and an iceberg is born. Icebergs might float in the ocean for many years. They might float for thousands of miles before they get to warmer water and begin to melt.

continued . . .

Many people worried about the danger of icebergs. When the ship Titanic hit an iceberg, people decided to do something. The International Ice Patrol was formed. The patrol watches for icebergs. They use radar, airplanes, and satellites to tell where icebergs are. The patrol can tell sailors how to sail around icebergs. Since the International Ice Patrol began, not one ship has hit an iceberg.

Main Idea
1. What are icebergs?

   _____

2. How are icebergs formed?

   _____

Significant Details
3. What are rivers of ice?

   _____

4. What happens when snow is packed together for many years?

   _____

5. Where can you find icebergs?

   _____

6. What is the International Ice Patrol? _____

7. The International Ice Patrol was founded when the
   a. first ship sank.
   b. Titanic sank.
   c. satellite sank.

8. Name two things the International Ice Patrol uses to detect icebergs.
   a. _____
   b. _____

Context Clues
9. *Crews* on the ships can't see underwater.
   a. sailors
   b. passengers
   c. decks

10. Icebergs *float* for several years.
    a. melt in water
    b. move in water
    c. freeze in water

Drawing Conclusions
11. Why did sailors hate icebergs?

    _____

12. Why wouldn't you find an iceberg near the desert? _____

    _____

Following Through
13. Do you think the International Ice Patrol does its job well? _____
    Why or why not? _____

    _____

    _____

    _____

Titanic

In the early 1900s, people who wanted to go between Europe and America often used ships. A new and beautiful ship, the Titanic, was ready in 1912. It had extra strong sides and many new improvements. The owners of the ship called it "unsinkable." That spring the Titanic left Europe on its first trip. It was going from London to New York City. The people on the ship were having a fine time.

All at once there was a crash! The ship had hit an iceberg. The iceberg had been sighted, but not in time. Water gushed into the boiler rooms and the ship began to tilt.

The people ran to the lifeboats. But then they made a terrible discovery. Since the owners of the ship thought it could never sink, they had not put on enough lifeboats for everyone. Only about 700 of the 2200 people aboard were able to fit in the lifeboats. Most of the 700 in lifeboats were rescued. But those left on the ship drowned in the icy water when the Titanic sank. People called this the worst sea disaster of the times.

The Titanic lay in the cold water at the bottom of the sea for over 70 years. Recently, American and French explorers were testing new equipment. They used an unmanned submarine that could take pictures underwater. After searching for two months, the team found the Titanic.

Everyone was excited about the discovery. A new submarine, called *Alphie,* took the explorers back for a closer look. *Alphie* gently glided around the rusted metal and huge anchor.

continued . . .

15

MP3388

The explorers were able to look inside the Titanic and see what was left.

Ten years later, a team of explorers tried to raise a piece of the ship's hull. The piece weighed nine tons! Just before it was pulled to the surface, the hull broke away and sank again.

Explorers were still able to learn a great deal about the Titanic. Everyone thought that the iceberg had cut a big hole in the ship and that's what made it sink. But searchers could not find any holes. They tested the steel from the hull of the ship. Scientists say that the hull was made of steel that wasn't strong enough for the bitter cold waters of the North Atlantic. They think the steel became brittle from the cold and just cracked easily when the ship bumped the iceberg.

Exploration of this sunken bit of history continues. Many things from the Titanic have been recovered. A two-foot bronze whistle from the smokestack was found. It still works! Some gold bars were found. Searchers think these might have been a payment for trade from London to the United States. But no one knows for sure. They are waiting for official records which cannot be opened until 2012.

Some things are known for sure. The United States government looked into the disaster. They made a rule saying that every U.S. ship must have enough lifeboats for everyone on board. Ships are sent on different routes to avoid icebergs. And an official is always listening, day and night, in case someone sends a distress signal. They hope to avoid any more disasters.

Main Idea

1. This story is about a

   _____.

2. Which sentence is most important in the story?
   a. The people were having a fine time.
   b. The Titanic is filled with treasure.
   c. All at once there was a crash.

Significant Details

3. Water came in through
   a. the lifeboats.
   b. a hole in the ship's side.
   c. a submarine.

4. The Titanic was finally found
   a. after a great search.
   b. by the air force.
   c. accidentally.

Context Clues

5. The ship began to *tilt*.
   a. tip on its side
   b. lose the lifeboats
   c. sail away

6. The owners thought the Titanic was *unsinkable*.
   a. It would never hit an iceberg.
   b. It would never sink.
   c. It would never sail.

Drawing Conclusions

7. What could have saved more lives when the Titanic sank?

   _____

8. Do you think the Titanic should stay at the bottom of the ocean? Why?

   _____
   _____
   _____

Gwendolyn Brooks

Young Gwendolyn Brooks was different from other girls and boys in her neighborhood. While the children were out playing, Gwendolyn was writing poetry.

Gwendolyn grew up in a black neighborhood near Chicago, Illinois. She wrote about growing up in the city. When she was 13, a children's magazine published one of her poems about her neighborhood.

Since then she has written many poems and books. *Bronzeville Boys and Girls* is a poetry book that Gwendolyn wrote for children. She got ideas for these poems from her own childhood. Her poem "Keziah" is about a secret hiding place. Gwendolyn had a secret hiding place when she was little. That was where she liked to write. "Rudolph Is Tired of the City" tells about a child who wants to push all the city buildings away. Gwendolyn probably felt that way in her crowded neighborhood. "Eppie" is about a little girl who wishes for something that is all her own.

Gwendolyn has won many awards for her poetry. The Pulitzer Prize is a special award given to the best writer. Gwendolyn Brooks was the first black writer to win that award for her poetry.

Gwendolyn still writes, but she now spends more time with other young writers. Gwendolyn opened her home as a place for young writers to work and live. She gives them good advice. She tells

continued . . .

new writers that the best things to write about are their own feelings and experiences. Gwendolyn is proud of her African American background. She talks about it in her own writing.

Gwendolyn Brooks became a professor of English at Chicago State University. There she works with beginning writers to discover their own identities through writing. Her own poems tell so much about her own identity. Her poems are still being enjoyed today.

Main Idea

1. Gwendolyn Brooks
   a. trains animals.
   b. writes poems.
   c. sings poetry.
2. Gwendolyn writes about
   a. building houses.
   b. children in school.
   c. growing up in the city.

Significant Details

3. Gwendolyn Brooks was the first black writer to
   a. win a Pulitzer Prize.
   b. write a poem.
   c. live in the city.
4. The poem "Keziah" is about
   a. a little boy.
   b. a dog.
   c. a secret hiding place.
5. Gwendolyn grew up near
   a. Cincinnati.
   b. Chicago.
   c. China.
6. Gwendolyn's first poem was published when she was
   a. 30.
   b. 7.
   c. 13.

Context Clues

7. Gwendolyn's poem was *published* in a magazine.
   a. printed for others to read
   b. written for herself
   c. put away
8. She won an *award* for her poetry.
   a. art contest
   b. punishment
   c. prize
9. She grew up in a black *neighborhood.*
   a. place where people live
   b. place where people go to school
   c. place where people write poetry

Drawing Conclusions

10. Do you think Gwendolyn enjoyed her childhood? Why or why not?

   _____

   _____

11. Why might it be a good idea for a writer to write about his or her own experiences?

   _____

   _____

Following Through

12. Find examples of Gwendolyn Brooks's or another poet's poetry. Copy one poem to share with a friend.

18   MP3388

Dressing a Japanese Tree

When it is cold outside, you wear a coat and hat. When it is cold in Japan, the trees wear coats and hats, too.

Almost every Japanese house has a garden. The Japanese think of gardens as part of their homes. They spend a lot of time to make them beautiful. The gardens are made to look like tiny worlds. A little pond in the garden stands for the ocean. Small hills stand for mountains. Trees and bushes stand for forests.

Japanese gardens are planned with care. They show how close the Japanese people are to nature. The gardens are built to be enjoyed in every season. Even the snow in winter is thought of as a flower called *toka.* The Japanese like to see the way snow lies on bare branches.

Long before the snow comes, Japanese gardeners get the plants ready for winter. In the western part of Japan, the winter snow is very heavy. Trees and bushes need to be protected.

In the fall, gardeners begin to make "coats" for the trees. The coats are made out of rice straw. A gardener starts at the trunk of the tree. He wraps straw around the bottom of the tree and ties it with a cord. Another layer of straw is wrapped around the tree and tied. The gardener wraps the tree until he reaches the top. Then he wraps the tree again. This time he starts at the top of the tree and wraps to the bottom. When he is finished, the gardener cuts all the edges of the straw to make a smooth coat. Sometimes more straw is tied together to make a "top hat."

continued . . .

19

MP3388

Little straw huts are built to protect small bushes and flowers. Sometimes these huts look like teepees. This way, plants have their own houses to keep them warm.

The trees wear their coats and hats until spring. This helps the natural beauty of a Japanese garden last a long time.

Main Idea
1. Japanese people take special care of their
   a. children.
   b. gardens.
   c. seasons.

Significant Details
2. A pond in a Japanese garden stands for _____ .
3. Snow in Japan is thought of as a
   _____ .
4. Small hills in a Japanese garden stand for _____ .
5. Coats for trees are made out of
   _____ .
6. Trees and bushes need to be protected from _____ .

Context Clues
7. The gardener put another *layer* of straw on the tree.
   a. Japanese flower
   b. another coat
   c. Japanese garden

8. The trees are *protected*.
   a. kept safe
   b. planned
   c. damaged
9. The *gardener* watered the flowers.
   a. a person who takes care of Japan
   b. person who sews coats and gloves
   c. person who takes care of plants

Drawing Conclusions
10. How can you tell that Japanese people are close to nature?
11. Would you like to visit a Japanese garden? Why or why not?

Following Through
12. There are gardens all over the world. Read about gardens and gardeners. Write briefly of something new you learn.

The Rice Crop
(Adapted from Lafacadio Hearn's *Gleanings in Buddha-Fields*)

Many years ago in Japan, there lived a kind, old man. He was called *Ojiisan*, the Japanese word for grandfather.

One day the people in the village below were having a party. Everyone's rice crop had grown well this year and the villagers were happy. Ojiisan stood in front of his house with his grandson, Tada. They could see the whole village, which stood next to the sea. Ojiisan smiled as he watched the villagers. He was glad everyone's rice crop had grown so well. His own rice fields were ready to be picked.

All at once, the ground started to shake! Probably just another one of Japan's mild earthquakes. But then a strange thing happened. The waves on the shore rolled *back* into the sea. Villagers ran to the shore to look at the sea.

Ojiisan's smile quickly disappeared. He knew something was wrong. "Hurry, Tada," he shouted. "Light a torch!" Tada quickly lit a torch. He handed it to his grandfather. Ojiisan took the torch and set his rice crop on fire.

"Oh grandfather! What are you doing?" sobbed Tada. "Please stop."

But Ojiisan wouldn't stop. He kept burning his fields until large clouds of black smoke rose to the sky.

The villagers saw the smoke and came running up the mountain to help. The people were worried about Ojiisan. Why was he acting so strangely? When the last villager was on the mountaintop, Ojiisan pointed to the sea.

continued . . .

A huge tidal wave, as tall as a cliff, came thundering onto the shore. Water sprayed everywhere. When the wave rolled back out to sea, the whole village was gone. The tidal wave had destroyed everything.

At first, no one on the mountain said anything. Then Ojiisan spoke. "That is why I set fire to my rice fields," he said. "There was no other way to warn you. I knew you would all come up to help me."

Main Idea
1. The main idea of this story is
   a. The villagers were celebrating because their rice crops had grown so well.
   b. Ojiisan was afraid of earthquakes.
   c. Ojiisan gave up something of his own to help other people.

Significant Details
2. Why did Ojiisan burn his rice fields? _____
3. The word *Ojiisan* means

   _____ .
4. The village stood next to the

   _____ .

Drawing Conclusions
11. What type of person do you think Ojiisan was? _____

_____

12. Do you think Ojiisan had good neighbors? Why or why not? _____

_____

13. What lesson can be learned from this story? _____

_____

14. Did this story have a happy or sad ending? Explain. _____

_____

_____

5. After the earthquake struck, the waves on shore _____ .
6. Tada was _____ .
7. When the villagers saw the smoke, they _____ .
8. The village was destroyed by a

   _____ .

Context Clues
9. The rice *crop* grew well.
   a. village by the sea
   b. plants grown in a field
   c. mountain
10. The *tidal wave* thundered onto the shore.
    a. waves made by an earthquake
    b. waves made by a large boat
    c. waves in Japan

Dinosaurs Print Their Story

Real dinosaurs could not smile or play like Dino of *The Flintstones* cartoons. But they could fly or run or walk. And scientists keep discovering more and more about these strange creatures.

At a new discovery spot in Canada, scientists found some very small dinosaur footprints in fossils. Because the prints were no bigger than a penny, the dinosaur must have been the size of a tiny bird.

Dinosaur footprints found in France show that some dinosaurs could jump! A left and a right footprint were found side by side. The next closest set of prints was found almost seven feet away. These prints show that some dinosaurs could jump over a child's head. Other prints have shown scientists that some dinosaurs could kick.

With such strong jumps and kicks, the dinosaurs could have had the most powerful karate team in the world!

Main Idea

1. This story is mostly about
   a. scientists.
   b. kicks.
   c. dinosaurs.

Significant Details

2. The smallest footprints were
   a. no bigger than a penny.
   b. found in France.
   c. discovered long ago.

3. Scientists think dinosaurs could
   a. think.
   b. dig.
   c. jump.

4. The tiny dinosaur footprints were found in a
   a. penny.
   b. fossil.
   c. hill.

Context Clues

5. *Karate* is a
   a. new dinosaur.
   b. sport.
   c. kick.

Drawing Conclusions

6. From the story, you can tell there is probably
   a. a karate team in France.
   b. a tiny bird in Canada.
   c. more to learn about dinosaurs.

Following Through

7. Find a large picture of your favorite dinosaur. Study its feet to understand how it moved. Do you think your favorite dinosaur could jump or kick? Why or why not?

The Shed

Maria first saw the shed the day her family moved into their new house. It leaned against a fence in the backyard. Dark vines almost covered the shed. Most of its white paint had fallen off. What was in it? Maria knew she had to find out.

But at lunch her mother said, "Maria, the last owners told me there is a strange, old shed in the yard. Do not go near it without me."

Maria tried to wait for her mother, but there was something about that shed! "I'll just take a quick look," thought Maria.

She went out the door and down to the shed. She pushed aside some vines. Maria had uncovered an old door with a huge, brass knob. She reached for the knob, and suddenly the door flew open! Maria gasped and jumped back. Oh, why hadn't she waited for her mother? Was it too late to close that door???

Finish the story. If necessary, continue on another page.

_____

_____

_____

_____

_____

_____

_____

_____

_____

_____

_____

_____

_____

_____

Around the World Voyages

Not since the Wright brothers made their first airplane flight had there been such excitement! Now the Rutan brothers were hoping to make history in the air. The Rutans built and flew the Voyager, a special type of airplane which would set a new world record.

It all started when Dick and Burt Rutan were having dinner with their friend, Jeana Yeager. Burt turned to Dick and asked, "Would you like to be the first to fly around the world without stopping for fuel?"

Dick and Jeana liked the idea. But it didn't seem possible. There wasn't a plane that could hold that much fuel.

Burt knew just how to build such a plane. He is the president of Rutan Aircraft Factory and has designed hundreds of planes. There in the restaurant, Burt drew his idea for the plane on a paper napkin.

Five years later that very same airplane sat on the airstrip at Edwards Air Force Base. Its two pilots, Dick Rutan and Jeana Yeager, were ready for take-off.

Dick had been a fighter pilot in Vietnam. Jeana held nine world flight records. They were ready for anything. The Voyager took off on December 14, 1986, and ran into bad weather. The pilots used all their skills and kept the plane on a smooth course. After nine days and nights of flying, Dick and Jeana were home again. They had flown 26,000 miles around the world without stopping. A new world record had been set!

Dick enjoyed the voyage so much that he wanted to try again. He continued working on planes. Over the years, Dick adjusted his plane so that it would be just right for a very long trip. He included new instruments that would help him stay in contact during a long trip. A long journey around the world was taken by Dick and another pilot. Dick thought the trip was good, but he still wanted to go again. This time Dick is trying to fly around the world in a hot-air balloon. He may set a new world record again.

Main Idea

1. What did Dick and Jeana do?
   a. designed 130 planes
   b. worked for the Space Program
   c. made the first round-the-world flight without refueling

Significant Details

2. No one had ever made a trip like this before because
   a. no one was brave enough.
   b. no plane held enough fuel.
   c. the Wright brothers crashed.

3. The Voyager was designed by
   a. Burt Rutan.
   b. Dick Rutan.
   c. Jeana Yeager.

Context Clues

4. The plane's *fuel* is
   a. gasoline.
   b. food.
   c. pilot.

Drawing Conclusions

5. Jeana Yeager was chosen to make the flight because
   a. it was her idea.
   b. she is a woman.
   c. she is an experienced pilot.

6. From the story, you can tell that
   a. Dick and Jeana had an easy flight.
   b. Dick and Jeana work well together.
   c. Burt does not like to fly.

The Wild One

What has a bright blue face, hair that stands straight up, and long, black eyelashes? Is it a punk rock star? No, guess again. It is a strange jungle bird, the hoatzin.

The hoatzin lives near rivers in South America. It is not like any other bird! A baby hoatzin has claws on the ends of its wings. It can crawl up and down a tree trunk to get to its nest. Sometimes a baby bird may fall into the water. But it can dive and swim underwater just like a fish. It can then return safely to the riverbank. Then, using its claws, legs, and bill, the bird can climb back to its nest.

As the bird gets older, the claws disappear, and the wings grow. A large sack, or crop, also grows inside the bird's chest. Hoatzins eat leaves, flowers, and sometimes fruit. A hoatzin can store large amounts of this food in its crop.

Hoatzins live in small friendly groups of about ten birds. They build nests from twigs. All of the older birds share in taking care of the young. Hoatzins may look and act strangely, but they are very good baby-sitters. Although they are in a class by themselves, scientists now think these strange birds may be distant cousins of the cuckoo.

Main Idea
1. The hoatzin
   a. is different from other birds.
   b. lives near the South Pole.
   c. does not like trees.

Significant Details
2. This bird has _____ on its wings when it is young.
   a. no feathers
   b. claws
   c. blue hair
3. The hoatzin likes to eat
   a. tree branches.
   b. leaves.
   c. bugs.

4. Which one may be a cousin to the hoatzin?
   a. cuckoo
   b. punk rock star
   c. fish

Context Clues
5. The claws *disappear*.
   a. get bigger
   b. get smaller
   c. go away
6. A hoatzin can *store* food in its crop.
   a. get rid of
   b. keep
   c. buy

26

MP3388

The Disappearing River

Deep in the dark jungles of Brazil lay a strange mystery. It was known as the River of Doubt. People in Brazil could see where the river started. No one knew where it ended. The thick jungle was too dangerous for most men. People thought the river just disappeared somewhere in the jungle.

Theodore Roosevelt, the 26th president of the United States, loved adventure. After he left office, he decided to solve the mystery of the disappearing river. On February 27th, 1914, Roosevelt, his son Kermit, and twenty other men set out in canoes on the River of Doubt.

For several days the men floated along peacefully. They enjoyed the beautiful wildlife around them. But the wildlife soon turned dangerous. Mosquitoes, snakes, and bugs bit the men and made them sick. Man-eating piranhas nipped at their toes.

The men's troubles continued. The quiet river turned into rapids. Several canoes were smashed to bits in the roaring water. Kermit's canoe overturned, and his partner drowned. Indians shot arrows at the men, killing their dog. Most of their food was gone.

Perhaps the people were right. Maybe there really *was* no end to this river. But Roosevelt, who was very sick with malaria, wanted to solve the mystery. After two months, the Roosevelt canoes finally came to the end of the river. The mystery was solved!

The River of Doubt simply flowed into another river called the Airapuana. Roosevelt and his men had successfully made it through the thousand-mile river. The Brazilian government renamed it the Roosevelt River.

Main Idea
1. Roosevelt solved the mystery of
   a. a cure for malaria.
   b. the end of the River of Doubt.
   c. a jungle in Brazil.

Significant Details
2. The River of Doubt flowed into
   a. the ocean.
   b. a lake.
   c. another river.

Context Clues
3. If you *doubt* something, you
   a. are not sure of it.
   b. have heard about it before.
   c. are able to prove it.

4. They enjoyed the *wildlife* around them.
   a. canoes
   b. arrows
   c. animals

Drawing Conclusions
5. The River was renamed because
   a. Roosevelt River is shorter.
   b. Roosevelt traveled it first.
   c. Roosevelt was president.

6. ___ men found the end of the river.
   a. Twenty
   b. Twenty-one
   c. Twenty-two

The Greedy Dog
(Adapted from Aesop's Fable *The Dog and His Shadow*)

Once there lived a big, brown dog. Every day he trotted down to the meat market. The man who ran the meat market was very friendly. He often gave leftover bones to the dogs in the neighborhood.

One morning the man had a very large bone. Hungrily, the big, brown dog snapped it up.

"I'm going to take this home and keep it all for myself," said the dog.

Off he went, clutching the bone between his teeth. He stayed on the back streets of town. He hoped no one would see him with his bone. He was afraid another dog would take it away from him.

But behind an old house he met a small, hungry puppy. The puppy was too little to look for food on its own. It sat up, licked its lips, and begged for some of the bone. But the big, brown dog chased the puppy away.

On the next street there lay a tired, old dog. He was very weak. He couldn't search for food by himself. He, too, begged for just a bite of the bone. But the brown dog growled at the tired, old dog and wouldn't share his bone with him.

To get home, the brown dog had to walk across a little bridge over a stream. As he crossed the bridge, the brown dog saw something very strange. There, in the clear stream, was another brown dog. It had a large bone in its mouth, too! In fact, when the water rippled, the bone in the stream looked even larger than his!

continued . . .

MP3388

"I'd like to take that bone home too," thought the dog. "Then I'll have two juicy bones all to myself. I'll just jump down on top of that other dog and grab its bone."

The greedy dog jumped off the bridge and into the water. But he couldn't find the second dog anywhere. The brown dog wasn't a very good swimmer. Soon he began to go under the water. He paddled and kicked and dropped his bone as he tried to get out of the stream.

Finally, the big brown dog made it to shore and lay there panting. He was tired and hungry. Instead of two big, juicy bones, this greedy dog had none.

Main Idea

1. What is the lesson to be learned in this story?
   a. Never dive into deep water.
   b. If you are tricky, you get more.
   c. Be satisfied with what you have.

Significant Details

2. Why didn't the brown dog share with the old dog?
   a. He was greedy.
   b. The old dog growled at him.
   c. The old dog wasn't hungry.

3. What happened to the brown dog's bone?
   a. He shared it.
   b. He ate it.
   c. He lost it in the river.

Context Clues

4. If you are *greedy*, you
   a. share with others.
   b. want more than you need.
   c. are hungry.

5. He was *clutching* the bone.
   a. swallowing
   b. dropping
   c. holding tightly

Drawing Conclusions

6. When he looked in the stream, the brown dog really saw
   a. a bigger dog.
   b. himself.
   c. a smaller dog.

7. If the brown dog gets another bone, he should
   a. hide it quickly.
   b. keep away from the stream.
   c. share it.

Following Through

Read more of Aesop's fables. Some titles of his fables are given in the next story.

The Story of Aesop

Long, long ago, there lived a dark-skinned little man. Iadmon, a rich Greek man, bought this little man and made him his slave. The Greeks called the little slave Ethiop, or Aesop. They thought all dark-skinned people were from Ethiopia, Africa.

Aesop was never sent to school. But he did learn a lot from Iadmon. Many important Greek men came to visit Iadmon. Aesop watched them closely. He began to make up stories about these people. Aesop did not use real people in his stories. He used animals.

Iadmon loved to listen to Aesop's stories. Each story told about an animal and ended with a lesson or moral. Iadmon often visited his wealthy friends. He took Aesop with him on these visits. Aesop delighted everyone with his stories.

Soon Aesop became very famous for his animal fables. As a reward, Iadmon set him free. Aesop was no longer a slave. He could go anywhere and tell his fables.

The Emperor Croesus heard about Aesop and called him to his palace. He had an important job for Aesop. He sent him to the city of Delphi with money for the people. Aesop went to Delphi and met the people. They were mean and fought among themselves. Aesop would not give these selfish people the money. They were very angry with Aesop and threw him over a cliff to his death.

continued . . .

MP3388

Aesop had never written down his stories. But people remembered them and told them over and over again. Some of the most well-known fables are: *The Tortoise and the Hare*, *The Goose That Laid the Golden Egg*, and *The Fox and the Grapes*. Many popular sayings have come from his fables. "Don't count your chickens before they hatch" is the lesson in *The Milkmaid and Her Pail*. "Look before you leap" is from *The Two Frogs*. "He is just crying wolf" is an expression from *The Boy Who Cried Wolf*.

Today, Aesop's fables are enjoyed by people in every country in the world.

Main Idea
1. This story is mostly about Aesop and his
   a. master.
   b. animals.
   c. storytelling.

Significant Details
2. Aesop learned a lot about people from
   a. going to school.
   b. listening and watching.
   c. Emperor Croesus.
3. All of Aesop's stories have
   a. a happy ending.
   b. many people.
   c. a lesson to be learned.
4. In his stories, Aesop told about
   a. animals.
   b. made-up names.
   c. slaves.

Context Clues
5. A *fable* is a
   a. slave.
   b. hard job.
   c. story with a lesson.

Drawing Conclusions
6. From the story, you can tell that Aesop
   a. was clever and sneaky.
   b. stood up for what he believed was right.
   c. wanted to make a lot of money.

Following Through
7. What do the sayings "Don't count your chickens before they hatch" and "Look before you leap" mean? Read Aesop's stories. Try to put these sayings into your own words.
8. Write your own fable. Be sure to include a moral at the end.

MP3388

The Marching Ducks

It is mid-morning at the Peabody Hotel in Memphis, Tennessee. Crowds of people have gathered in the hotel's fancy lobby. Excitement is in the air. A red carpet is rolled out from the elevators to the marble fountain in the middle of the lobby. Music plays over the loudspeakers. The elevator doors open. People lift their cameras.

Who is coming? Is it a movie star? A visiting king or queen? No, it is the Peabody Marching Ducks.

The Peabody Ducks have been putting on a show at the hotel for over fifty years. Every morning at eleven o'clock, the ducks proudly march in a parade across the lobby to their "swimming pool." They spend the day in the hotel fountain, splashing and swimming and posing for pictures.

People come from all over to the Peabody Hotel. They have come because of the famous ducks. And the ducks put on a good show.

Edward Pembroke has been training the ducks since 1940. He was once an animal trainer for Ringling Brothers' Circus. Mr. Pembroke spends each day with the ducks. They learn things quickly. They can march in a straight line. The ducks know his voice, and they listen for his commands. He also gives them signals with his cane.

Mr. Pembroke made the ducks fun to watch. He works with the ducks for three months at the Peabody. They are then sent back to their home on a farm. Then new ducks are chosen for the Peabody Marching Ducks.

There were ducks at the Peabody even before Mr. Pembroke. The hotel owner came back from a hunting trip with live ducks. He let the ducks swim in the hotel's fountain. They have been there ever since.

continued . . .

MP3388

These are truly "lucky ducks." After a long swim, the ducks climb out of the marble fountain. At five o'clock, they slowly march back to the elevator. Up they go to the Royal Duck Palace, their penthouse on the roof of the hotel. The palace is a special cage. It was made just for the ducks. It, too, has a fountain for swimming. Ducks don't like to walk on concrete, so the palace even has carpets. The ducks sleep in the "Royal Bedchamber," a fancy tent with a crown on top. Every morning they eat special food from the hotel's kitchen. Then they begin another day of marching and swimming for visitors.

A Peabody duck would probably say, "Life here is just ducky!"

Main Idea
1. This story is mostly about
   a. Edward Pembroke.
   b. visitors to the Peabody.
   c. the Peabody Ducks.
2. The ducks are famous because
   a. Tennessee has no ducks.
   b. the ducks march for people.
   c. they are good hunters.

Significant Details
3. The ducks live at the hotel
   a. for over fifty years.
   b. for three months.
   c. all their lives.
4. The Royal Bedchamber is a
   a. tent.
   b. carpet.
   c. fountain.

Context Clues
5. People waited in the hotel *lobby*.
   a. bedroom
   b. visitors' restaurant
   c. entrance
6. Mr. Pembroke *trains* the ducks.
   a. sells
   b. catches
   c. teaches them tricks

Drawing Conclusions
7. From the story, you can tell that Mr. Pembroke probably likes his job because
   a. he has been doing it since 1940.
   b. he gets to sleep in a Royal Bedchamber.
   c. he is paid well.

The Dancing Ghost

When I was little, my family often visited my grandparents in the country. These trips were very special to me. Grandma and Grandpa did everything the old-fashioned way. Grandma washed all her clothes in a big washtub in the backyard. She hung the clothes to dry on a clothesline. After dinner, Grandpa always made a batch of homemade ice cream. We all took turns adding rock salt and cranking the handle. We cranked until the batch was sweet and creamy.

One winter night we were just finishing our ice cream. Suddenly a huge storm arose. The sky turned black and thunder clapped loudly above us. Grandpa said, "This is a great time to tell one of my spooky ghost stories." I loved Grandpa's stories. My little brother and sister did not. They were easily scared.

Grandpa was telling us about a strange ghost. He came to town just once a year. The ghost banged on a drum until everyone in town woke up. Just then we heard a banging noise outside. The rain was pouring down, and the wind was blowing hard. No one wanted to go out and check the noise.

"It's the ghost!" my little sister cried. "He's banging on his drum!"

"There is no such thing," I tried to tell her.

"My lands!" called Grandma, looking out the kitchen window. "It *is* a ghost!"

We all ran to the window. There in the backyard was a headless ghost. Its white arms were outstretched, and its legs were kicking in the air.

Now my brother and sister were both crying. I wasn't really scared until I saw Grandpa get his rifle out of the closet. He stepped out on the back porch and shot his rifle at the ghost. But the ghost kept dancing right before our eyes. Grandpa shot again. One of the ghost's arms fell to its side. Grandpa shot again and again. Finally, the ghost lay in a heap in the backyard. *continued . . .*

34

MP3388

The wind and the rain were still very strong. We decided to wait until morning to go look at the ghost. My little brother and sister crawled into bed with me that night. We lay there shaking and shivering all night. None of us could sleep.

The next morning was sunny and bright. Grandpa said that we all got up with the chickens. We couldn't wait to run out to the backyard.

The ghost still lay where it had fallen the night before. Grandma was standing over it, laughing and laughing.

"Grandpa," she called. "You shot your long underwear! Look—it's full of holes!" The "ghost" we had seen was only Grandpa's long white underwear. It had been hanging on the clothesline. The "drum" was Grandma's washtub, banging against the fence in the wind.

Grandpa still loves to tell his ghost stories. But now he has a new story to tell. No one gets scared when he tells about the dancing ghost. We all just laugh and laugh.

Main Idea
1. This story shows that
   a. ghosts always wear white.
   b. ghosts never bang drums.
   c. things are not always what they seem.

Significant Details
2. The banging noise was really
   a. the washtub.
   b. the ghost's drum.
   c. Grandpa's rifle.
3. The weather that night was
   a. snowy.
   b. stormy.
   c. clear.

Context Clues
4. The ghost's arms were *outstretched.*
   a. outside
   b. too long for his body
   c. reaching out at both sides

5. They got up *"with the chickens."*
   a. early
   b. late
   c. cackling

Drawing Conclusions
6. From the story, you might guess that
   a. Grandma and Grandpa believe in ghosts.
   b. Grandpa never got frightened in a storm.
   c. Grandpa and Grandma often had ghosts in their backyard.
7. The dancing ghost never returned to Grandpa's house. Why not?
   a. Grandpa shot it.
   b. There was never a real ghost.
   c. The ghost probably took his drum to a new town.

MP3388

Natural Art

"Busy as a bee" has a lot of meaning for sculptor Garnett Puett. Many sculptors carve a statue from wood or stone. Others shape clay into molds. The molds are then filled. The molds are broken away and a statue remains. But Puett has a new idea. He uses bees to help make statues.

They are not special bees. These bees are found in fields and gardens. First, Puett makes an outline of a person from wood and metal. Then, he coats the figure with sugar water. A queen bee is put into the middle of the shape. Then work is ready to begin.

Bees start to add a honeycomb to the frame. Hour after hour the bees bring nectar to the sculpture. They seem to naturally build things evenly. The bees add two inches of honeycomb to the right side of the head. Then they add two inches to the left. Soon the shape looks like a person. Often the bees' work makes a figure like an Egyptian mummy.

Puett watches the work of the bees day by day. Usually, he lets them build in their own way. But sometimes he may not like the shape of the beeswax. Puett can melt off the unwanted part. He then lets the bees begin again.

In a London art show, one of the beeswax figures held a real hive at its side. In a Chicago show, the figure was in a glass box. Bees came in and out of a hole in the museum wall.

continued . . .

MP3388

Bees finished the statue as people watched. In a St. Louis outdoor sculpture park, the bees were right at home. They found nectar in the nearby flowers. There they worked on a figure of the sculptor's wife.

Puett truly likes bees. He has studied their ways. He admires their hard work. With these statues, Puett can combine two of his favorite things. And the art world is positively buzzing about this exciting new idea in sculpture!

Main Idea

1. Garnett Puett
   - a. makes statues.
   - b. plays the piano.
   - c. draws cartoons.
2. _____ help Puett finish his art work.
   - a. Museums
   - b. Flowers
   - c. Bees

Significant Details

3. Puett coats a figure with
   - a. flowers.
   - b. sugar water.
   - c. wood.
4. If Puett does not like the work, he
   - a. melts the wax.
   - b. gets very angry.
   - c. throws it against the wall.

5. The Chicago show was in a
   - a. garden.
   - b. museum.
   - c. hall.

Context Clues

6. *Nectar* used by bees is found in the middle of flowers.
   - a. a bud
   - b. a kind of glue
   - c. a sweet liquid
7. Puett *combines* two of his favorite things.
   - a. mixes
   - b. fights against
   - c. orders

Drawing Conclusions

8. Do you think other sculptors will use bees? Explain. _____
   _____
   _____

The Lost Continent

When ancient Greeks taught their children about the world, they often used make-believe stories. These stories are called myths. There is one myth in ancient history which some people say may be true. The story was written by Plato, the well-known Greek teacher. It is about the lost continent of Atlantis.

Long ago, there was a very large island somewhere in the middle of the Atlantic Ocean. In fact, it was larger than Asia and Africa put together. This beautiful island was called Atlantis. Poseidon, the god of the sea, was its first king. Poseidon named the continent after his oldest son, Atlas.

Atlantis was a perfect place. It had lush, green forests, clear, blue lakes, tall mountains, and many birds and animals. The weather was good all year round, and there was plenty to eat.

Atlantis was a powerful empire. All of its people worked well together for everything they needed. The laws and rules in Atlantis were the best in the world.

But as time went by, some of the people changed. They fought with each other. They formed armies to take over other lands. No one obeyed the rules.

All of this made the mythical gods angry. Poseidon was sent to punish the people. One day there was a huge explosion in the sea. Mountains of waves crashed over Atlantis. By nightfall, the whole continent of Atlantis was covered by rushing waves. The large island sank to the bottom of the sea.

continued . . .

38

MP3388

Most people say that Atlantis never existed. But today some scientists are trying to prove that Atlantis was a real continent and still lies at the bottom of the ocean. They have found rock formations and pieces of land which they say prove their story.

Is Atlantis real or make-believe? We may have a chance to find out. Some scientists predict that one day Atlantis will rise again!

Main Idea
1. Atlantis was
   a. a continent.
   b. a god.
   c. an ocean.
2. Atlantis was destroyed because
   a. people in Asia and Africa took over the land.
   b. Poseidon was a bad king.
   c. the people of Atlantis acted poorly.

Significant Details
3. A myth is a
   a. Greek teacher.
   b. make-believe story.
   c. continent.
4. Atlantis was known around the world for its
   a. rushing waves.
   b. fair laws and rules.
   c. armies.

Context Clues
5. Atlantis was a powerful *empire*.
   a. place with a strong government
   b. place with beautiful weather
   c. an island in Greece

Drawing Conclusions
6. Atlantis may not be just a myth because
   a. Plato was a well-known teacher who never made up stories.
   b. the continent never sank. It is now known as Asia.
   c. scientists have discovered rock formations in the ocean which they think are from Atlantis.

Following Through
7. Check out a book of Greek mythology. Read other stories about rulers, gods, and Greek heroes.

MP3388

Saint George and the Dragon
(A legend adapted from Spenser's *Faerie Queen*)

George, Knight of England, rode through the forest to his first battle. He was looking for a terrible dragon. It was killing people and tearing up crops in a nearby country. Una, a beautiful princess from that country, had asked for his help. She rode with George to show him the way to the monster.

At last they came to the top of a hill. There, in the valley below, lay a huge dragon. It gave a terrible roar when it saw George. Then the dragon charged. The ground shook. The dragon's tail swished from side to side. Fire poured from its nose and mouth.

George raised his spear and rode down the hill. The spear struck against the dragon's side with a crash! The battle had begun! George and the dragon fought for three days. On the first day, George broke one of the dragon's wings with his spear. On the second day, the dragon held George tightly in its tail. George pulled out his sword and cut off the end of that big tail. On the third day, the tired dragon charged again at George. Fire poured from its open mouth. George covered his face and drove his sword straight into the dragon's mouth. The fierce monster crashed to the ground. All was still. The wicked dragon was dead!

George married the beautiful princess. He fought and won many other battles to help people in England. Soon he became known as Saint George, Defender of England.

Main Idea
1. In the story George
   a. tore up the crops.
   b. killed the dragon.
   c. asked for help.

Significant Details
2. Who asked for George's help?
   a. Princess Una
   b. people of the countryside
   c. King of England
3. George broke the dragon's wing
   a. with a sword.
   b. with fire.
   c. with a spear.

4. Fire poured from
   a. the dragon's mouth.
   b. the top of the hill.
   c. the tail of the dragon.

Context Clues
5. *Fierce* means the same as
   a. happy
   b. slow.
   c. wild.

Drawing Conclusions
6. George was
   a. big and boastful.
   b. brave and strong.
   c. fierce and mean.

Great Grizzlies

Once, long ago, giant grizzly bears roamed the West. They lived in the mountains and wilderness of California, Wyoming, and Montana. They also lived in Alaska and Canada.

But farmers began to settle in California and Montana. The farmers were afraid the grizzlies would hurt them and eat their farm animals. These settlers began to kill the grizzly bears. Once there were thousands of grizzly bears. Now there are only a few hundred. Most grizzlies now live in Alaska where they have more room to roam.

Early settlers had good reason to be afraid of the grizzlies. These big, brown bears are some of the biggest and strongest animals in America. Most weigh about 400–500 pounds. The strong muscles in their front paws and legs make these bears deadly fighters. Their powerful jaws can bite an animal and break its bones. They are fast runners and can catch their prey easily.

But grizzly bears aren't really the terrible killers that everyone thinks they are. They're just hungry. Grizzlies need to eat about 90 pounds of food a day! They must store this food for the winter months. Bears hibernate in the winter. Instead of looking for food, they live off their stored body fat. They depend on the food they ate during the warm months.

Grizzlies really like to eat plants more than animals. About 200 different plants, berries, and roots are favorites of the bears. Grizzlies in Alaska get a special treat. Each year, grizzlies meet at rivers to go fishing. Salmon is their favorite fish. When the salmon swim upstream to lay eggs, the grizzlies are waiting to catch the salmon with their teeth.

Recently, people have become interested in grizzly bears and want to save the bears from extinction. Some people are trying to bring more grizzlies back into their old areas. They are hoping that people won't be so afraid of them. Scientists say that the grizzly is really afraid of humans!

Main Idea

1. This story is mainly about
   a. wild animals in the wilderness.
   b. salmon fishing in Alaska.
   c. large, brown bears.

Significant Details

2. Grizzly bears have powerful
   a. jaws.
   b. eyesight.
   c. feet.

3. Grizzlies would rather eat
   a. people.
   b. meat.
   c. plants.

4. Many grizzlies were killed by
   a. freezing winters.
   b. farmers.
   c. animals.

Context Clues

5. Grizzly bears *roamed* the West.
   a. wandered about
   b. hunted in
   c. lived in

6. Grizzlies *hibernate* in winter.
   a. stay in a sleeping state
   b. travel to warmer climates
   c. look for new food

Grizzly Rescues

Grizzly bears are in danger. They might become extinct. That is, the last of the grizzly bears might die. There would be no new grizzly bears to carry on.

For years, people who were afraid of grizzly bears tried to kill them. Many grizzlies in California and other western states have been shot.

Luckily, scientists and others want to help the big brown beast. Scattered across the northwest are groups of people who want to protect the remaining grizzlies. Rescue stations are set up deep in the woods. Volunteers watch for grizzlies and help them stay safe.

A group of helpers in California want to bring the grizzly bear back into their valley. Each year they bring back one or two grizzlies. It is hoped that soon these bears will have cubs of their own, and the grizzly bear family will grow.

A group of Boy Scouts in Montana is really working to save the grizzly. They collect twigs, roots, and other natural materials. Then they dig small dens and cover them with the natural material.

These little dens are for homeless cubs. Mother bears push their cubs out after a few years. Sometimes cubs aren't ready to be on their own. They don't know how to build a den. They don't know how to prepare for hibernation. The Boy Scouts gather the motherless cubs and pack them away into the man-made dens. The cubs are able to hibernate and grow. Next year they will roam on their own.

Scientists in Wyoming wanted to know more about the grizzly bear. Workers put a collar around a sleeping bear's neck. Tiny radios are in the collars. When the bear wakes up and walks away, scientists can tell where it goes. The radios in the collars send messages back to the scientists. Scientists studied the bears from a long distance. They learned what bears ate and where they slept. They learned how bears got along with each other and who were the bears' enemies.

With the help of caring people, the grizzly may survive in the west. Man and beast will learn how to share the land. The great brown bear will roam again.

Main Idea

1. The grizzly bears are in danger because
   a. there is no where for them to live.
   b. there are not many grizzlies left.
   c. scientists are trying to shoot the bears.

Significant Details

2. Grizzlies live in the
   a. southwest part of the U.S.
   b. northwest part of the U.S.
   c. midwest part of the U.S.

3. Boy Scouts are helping
   a. scientists.
   b. mother bears.
   c. motherless bears.

4. A bear's collar acts like a
   a. radio.
   b. warm scarf.
   c. necklace.

Context Clues

5. Bears might become *extinct.*
   a. no longer living
   b. hunted
   c. saved

Drawing Conclusions

6. What might happen to the motherless cubs without the help of the Scouts?

   _____

   _____

Jungle Spirit
A Retelling of a Brazilian Folktale

Nights can be hot and humid in the jungles of Brazil. Families often sit outside to cool off. They tell stories far into the night. The children love to hear folktales and legends. A favorite tale is the story of the jungle spirit. Grown-ups sometimes tell the story so that their children will stay out of the jungle.

If you lived in the jungle, you would be warned about the inhambu. He is a jungle spirit in the shape of a large bird. You must watch out for the inhambu. He must not catch you. If he does, the inhambu could steal your shadow. Jungle people believed that if your shadow was stolen, you would get sick or die.

Years ago, the jungle was full of diseases. There was no medicine to cure these diseases. If one person got sick, the sickness could spread through the whole village. Many people died. People didn't know that some jungle bugs could make them sick. They didn't know that mosquito bites could kill them. Villagers wanted to blame the diseases on somebody. They blamed the inhambu.

The inhambu could be very tricky. He could take your shadow and hide it. He could squeeze your shadow into small spaces. You were lucky if you found your shadow again. Then you would not get sick. But if the inhambu was angry, he might steal your shadow and drown it in the river. The inhambu could reach out and cut your shadow with a wave of his arm. It was hard to get away from the inhambu.

The villagers believed there were many other evil spirits in the jungle. Some of them could steal your shadow, too. But only one spirit made everyone fearful. The spirit of inhambu was the most evil of all!

Main Idea
1. People in Brazil's jungles like to
   a. catch evil spirits.
   b. pass on folktales.
   c. stay up all night.
2. The inhambu is
   a. evil.
   b. a shadow.
   c. thoughtful.

Significant Details
3. The inhambu takes the shape of
   a. a villager.
   b. a shadow.
   c. a bird.
4. The inhambu would
   a. kill you.
   b. steal your shadow.
   c. cure your sickness.

5. You might not die if
   a. you fed the spirit.
   b. you found your shadow.
   c. you lost your shadow.

Context Clues
6. You would be *warned* about the spirit.
   a. be told about danger
   b. be involved with the spirit
   c. be told a lie

Drawing Conclusions
7. Why would children stay out of the jungle when their parents told them this story?_____

_____

8. Why might the villagers blame their sicknesses on a spirit?_____

_____

_____